PRETTY PROMISES

SHANOVIA LUMPKIN

Published by True Beginnings Publishing.
Copyright by Shanovia Lumpkin, 2021.

Pretty Promises, by Shanovia Lumpkin. © Copyright 2021. All Rights Reserved and Preserved. No part of this book may be reproduced or transmitted in any form or by any means, electronic or mechanical, including photocopying, recording, or by information storage and retrieval systems or other electronic or mechanical methods, without written permission of the Author with exceptions as to brief quotes, references, articles, reviews and certain other noncommercial uses permitted by copyright law. For permission requests, write to the Publisher, addressed "Attention: Permissions," at the address below.

true_beginnings_publishing@yahoo.com

Formatting, Editing, and all artwork by True Beginnings Publishing. All Illustrations, Cover Art, and text are Copyright Protected.

ISBN-13: 978-1-947082-19-9

Ordering Information:
To order additional copies of this book, please visit Amazon or the Author's website at: https://priceless-treasures.org/

This book is a compilation of affirmations by the Author. All quotes, thoughts, and writings are products of the Author's imagination. Any resemblance to actual events or persons, living or dead, is entirely coincidental. The quotes, thoughts, and writings are copyrighted to the Author and are protected under US Copyright law. Any theft of the Author's work will be prosecuted to the full extent of the law.

Pretty Promises.
© Shanovia Lumpkin.
First Printing, 2021.

~Dedication~

To my "pretty girl," Journee. Continue to be a sweet, talented, and genuine spirit.

To every little girl, adolescent, young adult, and women alike. These affirmations are promises of progress, prospective, and power created for the declaration of life unto you.

~Scripture~

"Death and life are in the power of the tongue, and those who love it will eat its fruit."
~Proverbs 18:21 New King James Version

~Quote~

"As a pretty girl thinks, speaks, feels, and does, she will be." **_PricelessTreasures**

~Table of Contents~

- **Introduction**
- **Parent:** *Affirm me from A-Z: "From me to you"*
- **Daughter:** *"I am what I say I am"*
- **Reminder:** *"Always believe in yourself"*

~<u>Introduction</u>~

Affirm yourself and your children. Get in the habit of speaking life, healing, prosperity, love, and growth into your life. It is important for parents to create a new generation of beautiful beings by constructing the words that will build up our youth from birth to adulthood.

One's words are powerful; strong enough to build empires as well as bring down kingdoms. So be mindful when you part your lips. Only speak with pure intent. Speak love, light, and progress into the atmosphere. Be a part of the change you wish to see. Moreover, if you cannot, hold your tongue. Tame those impure thoughts so that they may not spill over into the universe.

As you go through this book, feel free to color the letters of the alphabet as you think about the words associated with them. Think about it, say it aloud, and use colors that make you feel positive about the words and yourself. Write notes in the extra space. Think of different ways to say these important things to yourself. Be brave. Be bold. And have fun.

Affirm me From A-Z: "From Me To You"

Pretty Promises

You are
Ambitious and Authentic.

Shanovia Lumpkin

**You are
Bold and Beautiful.**

Pretty Promises

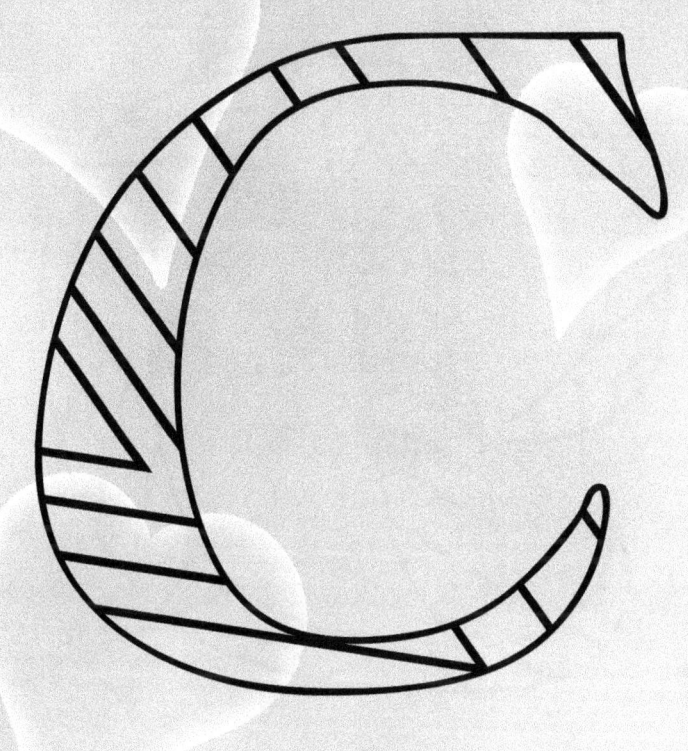

**You are
Caring, Charismatic,
Consistent, and Confident.**

Shanovia Lumpkin

You are
Discerning, Determined,
and Disciplined.

Pretty Promises

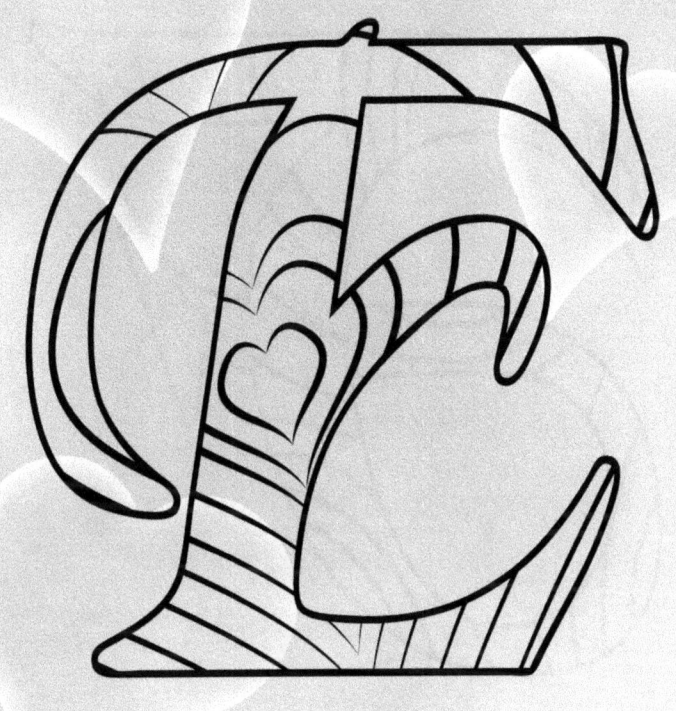

You are
Efficient and Enough.

Shanovia Lumpkin

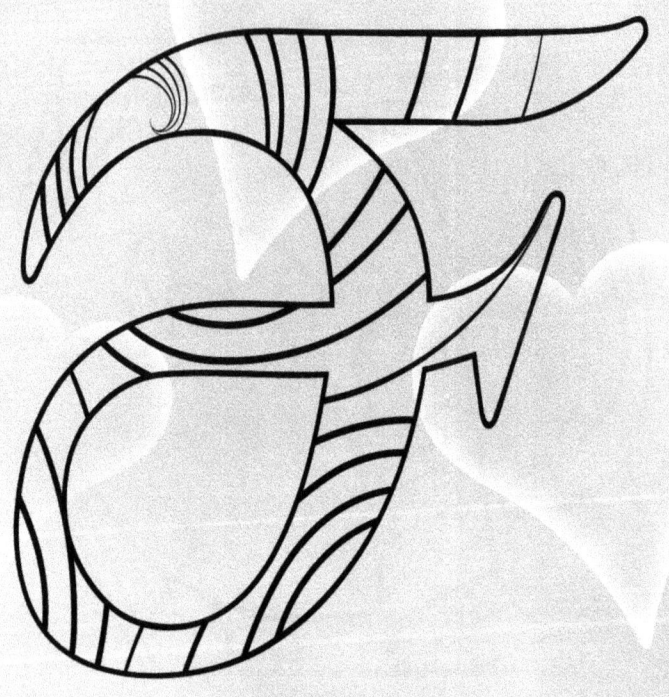

**You are
Focused and Fearless.**

Pretty Promises

**You are
Genuine and Generous.**

Shanovia Lumpkin

**You are
Honest, Helpful,
and Harmonious.**

Pretty Promises

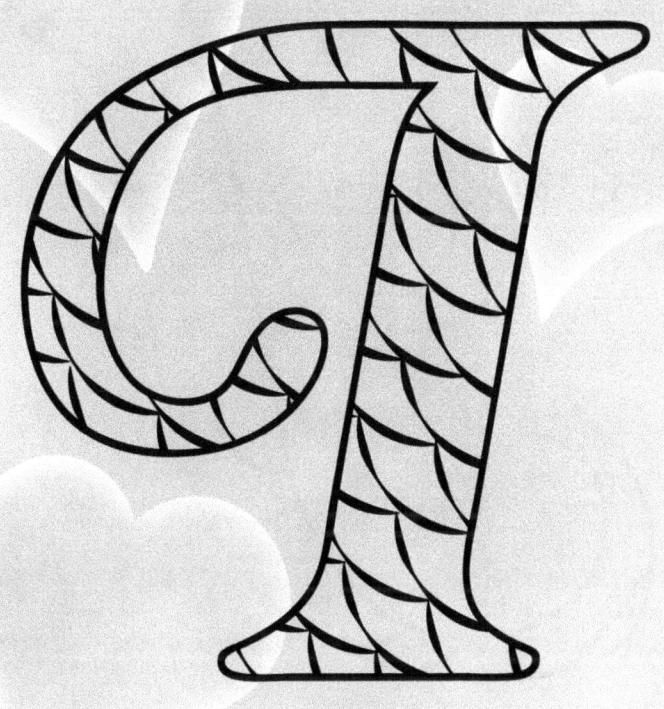

**You are
Insightful and Innovative.**

Shanovia Lumpkin

**You are
Joyful and Just.**

Pretty Promises

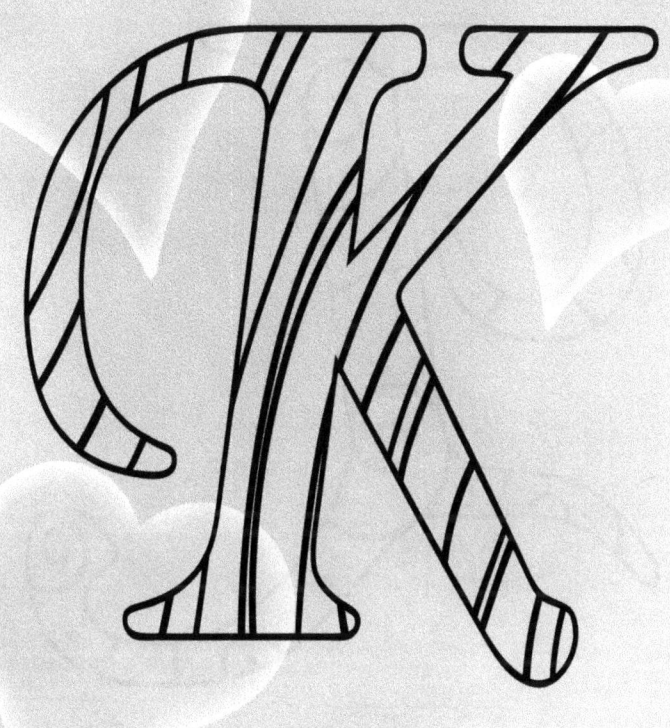

**You are
Kindhearted.**

Shanovia Lumpkin

**You are
Loving, Loveable,
and Loyal.**

Pretty Promises

**You are
Motivated and Majestic.**

Shanovia Lumpkin

**You are
Neat, Notorious,
and Nice.**

Pretty Promises

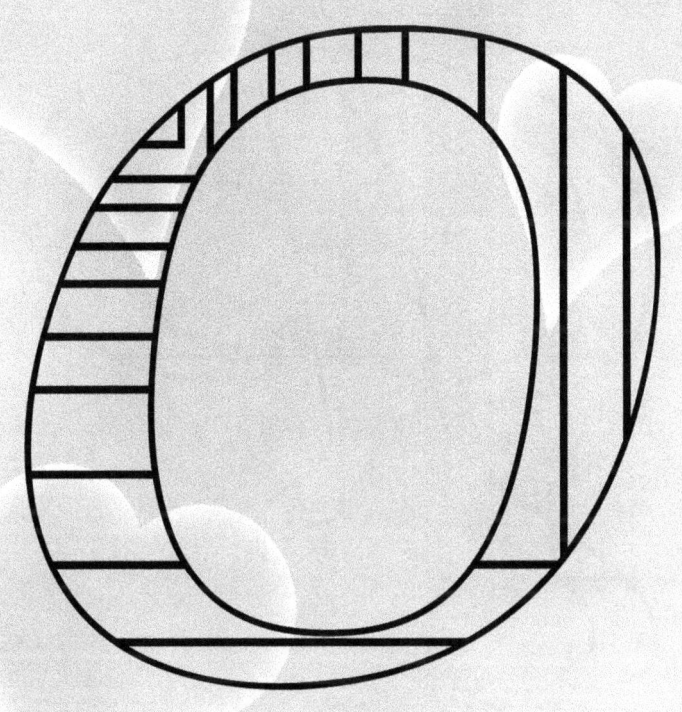

**You are
Obedient
and Openminded.**

Shanovia Lumpkin

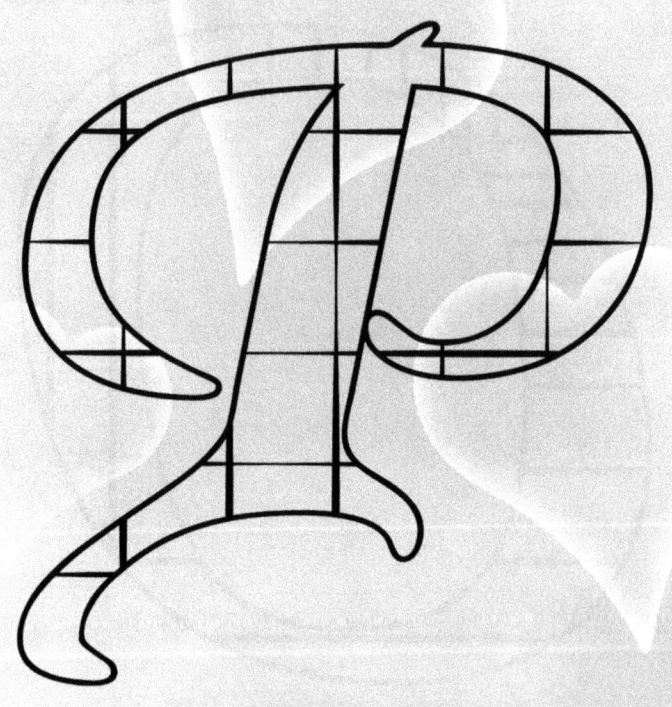

**You are
Powerful, Patient,
and Peaceful.**

Pretty Promises

**You are
Queenly.**

Shanovia Lumpkin

**You are
Respectful, Responsible,
Reliable, Radiant,
Resilient, and Resourceful.**

Pretty Promises

You are Sacred, Sweet, and Smart.

Shanovia Lumpkin

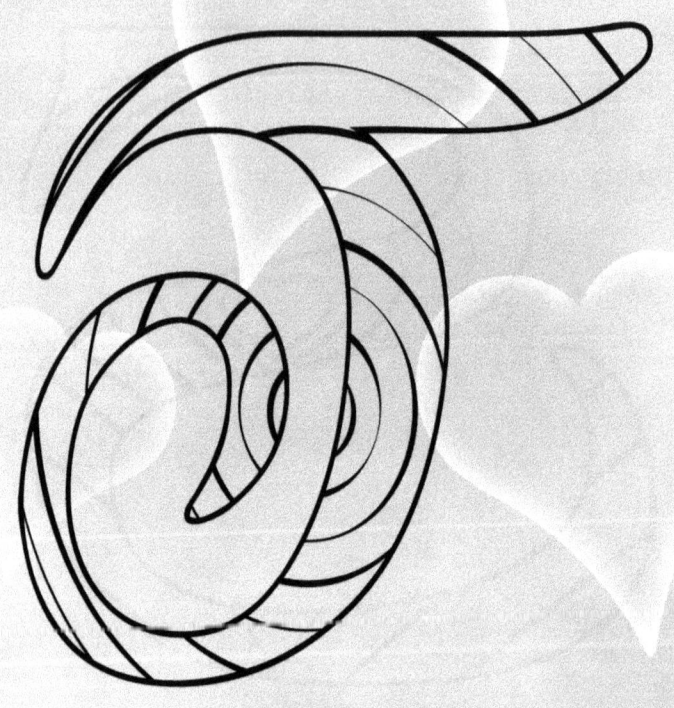

**You are
Trustworthy
and Talented.**

Pretty Promises

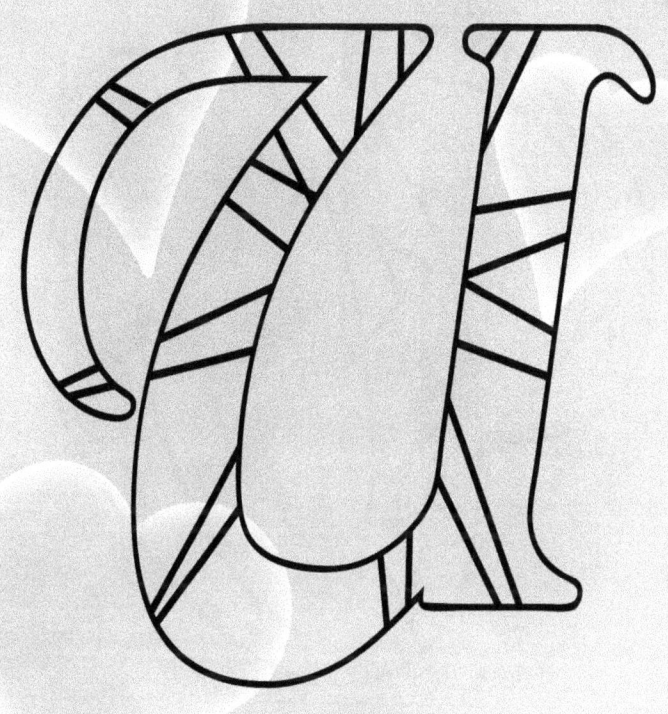

**You are
Unbreakable
and Undefeated.**

Shanovia Lumpkin

**You are
Vibrant, Valuable,
Versatile, and Victorious.**

Pretty Promises

You are
Worthy, Wise,
and Wonderfully Made.

Shanovia Lumpkin

**You are
a Xena.**

Pretty Promises

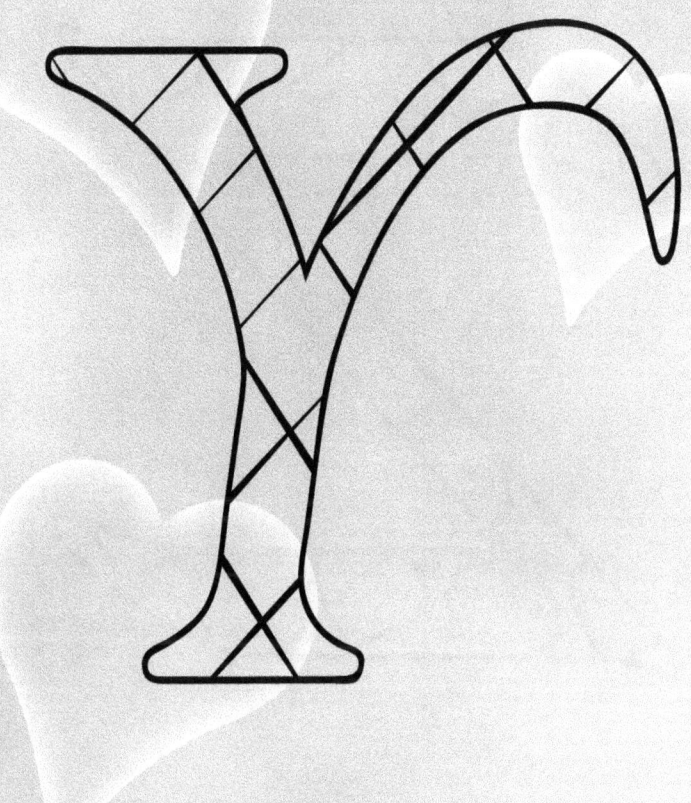

You are Youthful.

Shanovia Lumpkin

**You are
Zen.**

Pretty Promises

"I Am What I Say I Am"

Shanovia Lumpkin

I Am Strength

Pretty Promises

I Am Smart

Shanovia Lumpkin

I Am Beautiful

Pretty Promises

I Am Creative

Shanovia Lumpkin

I Am Healthy

Pretty Promises

I Am Wealthy

Shanovia Lumpkin

I Am
A Star

Pretty Promises

I Am
A Queen
In Training

Shanovia Lumpkin

I Am Talented

Pretty Promises

I Am
A Leader

Shanovia Lumpkin

I Am Special

Pretty Promises

I Am Important

Shanovia Lumpkin

I Am Respectful

Pretty Promises

I Am Polite

Shanovia Lumpkin

I Am Giving

Pretty Promises

I Am Loving

Shanovia Lumpkin

I Am Kind

Pretty Promises

I Follow Directions

Shanovia Lumpkin

I Am Focused

Pretty Promises

I Am
A Good
Listener

Shanovia Lumpkin

I Am Determined

Pretty Promises

I Am Love

Shanovia Lumpkin

I Am Light

Pretty Promises

I Am Positive Energy

Shanovia Lumpkin

I Am
A Good Person

Pretty Promises

I Have
A Good Heart

Shanovia Lumpkin

I Deserve The Best

Pretty Promises

I Will Treat Others The Way I Want To Be Treated

Shanovia Lumpkin

I Believe In Myself

Pretty Promises

"Always Believe In Yourself"

Shanovia Lumpkin

"I can't" is not a part of my vocabulary.

Pretty Promises

I can do anything I set my mind to do.

Shanovia Lumpkin

"It is too hard" doesn't pertain to me.

Pretty Promises

Because if I practice, take my time, and try my hardest, I will get it done.

Shanovia Lumpkin

I will not give up.

Pretty Promises

I will not give in.

Shanovia Lumpkin

I will succeed.

Pretty Promises

I will always win.

~About The Author~

Shanovia Lumpkin, also known as Priceless Treasure, is a freelance writer born and raised in Miami Florida where she learned the value of an education at a very young age. As a graduate from Miami Norland Senior High School, Shanovia developed a keen interest in expressive writing, which became evident in the eloquence of her poetry.

It was then that Priceless Treasure found her inner strength and self-awareness that propelled her into a life of abundance through vigilant affirmations and prayer.

"Priceless Treasures" is her first published book.

You can also find the Author in these places:

~**Website**~ ~**Twitter**~ ~**Instagram**~
priceless-treasures.org @PricelessT21588 _pricelesstreasures

~**Email**~ ~**Tumblr**~
shanovianicole@gmail.com priceless-treasures.tumblr.com

~**Facebook**~
www.facebook.com/PricelessTreasuresShanoviaLumpkin

www.ingramcontent.com/pod-product-compliance
Lightning Source LLC
Chambersburg PA
CBHW070101100426
42743CB00012B/2624